This book belongs to

Joy Lorraine Osborne

WISE WORDS for little people

KENNETH N. TAYLOR

Illustrated by Kathryn E. Shoemaker

TYNDALE HOUSE PUBLISHERS, INC.   WHEATON, ILLINOIS

OTHER BOOKS IN THIS SERIES

Big Thoughts for Little People

Giant Steps for Little People

All Scripture verses in this book are from
The Living Bible, copyright 1971 by Tyndale House Publishers.

First printing, October 1987

Library of Congress Catalog Card Number 87-51056
ISBN 0-8423-8232-1
Text, copyright 1987 by Kenneth N. Taylor
Artwork, copyright 1987 by Kathryn E. Shoemaker
Printed in the United States of America

A WORD TO PARENTS (and Grandparents)

The Bible's proverbs contain great truths that even small children need to know. Some proverbs are easier than others to understand and apply to a child's world. I have carefully selected some of these and made them live for today. As with each of the other books in this series, my prayer is that very young lives will be directed toward godly living. This small book, containing God's Word, can have a life-changing effect. I hope you will pray that the Spirit of God will take the message of each page and plant it deep in your child's heart.

KENNETH N. TAYLOR

P.S. Don't forget to look for the ladybugs in every picture!

Here's a secret you should know
To make your friends feel glad.
Just tell them all how nice they are,
And then they can't be sad!

Has anyone ever told you how good you look, or said something else nice about you? If so, I think you liked hearing it. It makes us feel good when someone says something nice about us. We should remember to say nice things about others, too. In this picture the children are helping each other and saying, "You ski very well. You look great." They are making each other feel good. God doesn't want us to say bad things about people, but to make them happy instead. I hope you will be like the children in the picture.

SOME QUESTIONS TO ANSWER
1. Can you think of something nice to say about someone you know? (Maybe it will be your father or mother or your friend or brother or sister.)
2. Did it make you feel good to say something nice about that person?

A LITTLE PRAYER
Thank you, God, for my friends. Help me to encourage them by saying kind things about them.

A BIBLE VERSE FOR YOU TO LEARN
The Lord delights in kind words. PROVERBS 15:26

Shadow is a guinea pig
That likes to run and play.
Keri is in charge of it;
She feeds it every day.

How many pets can you see in the picture? Pets are a lot of fun, but they can't take care of themselves. Do you know that God wants us to take care of our pets? He doesn't want us to forget to feed them or to clean their cages or give them water. That would be mean and cruel. God is happy when we are kind to animals. He made them, and he wants us to take care of them for him. Are you a good "taker-carer" of your pets? I hope so.

SOME QUESTIONS TO ANSWER
1. Do you have a pet? What is its name?
2. Can you remember a time when you forgot to take care of your pet? Was it sad? What did it say?
3. Is God happy when you take care of your pet?

A LITTLE PRAYER
Dear God, thank you for making my pets. Help me to take good care of them.

A BIBLE VERSE FOR YOU TO LEARN
Good people are concerned for the welfare of their animals. PROVERB

Jenny said, "Don't help me!"
As she started down the stairs.
But then they all went flying—
All her toys and little bears.

A little girl named Jenny thought she knew everything. She didn't want anybody to give her advice. She would say, "Don't help me, I'm big. I can do it all by myself." One day Jenny tried to take a wagon downstairs. Her mother had warned her not to do it, but she wouldn't listen. Now look what happened. I'm glad Jenny wasn't hurt, but she should have listened to her mother. God wants us to listen to what our friends and parents think is best for us. It is foolish not to listen to good advice.

SOME QUESTIONS TO ANSWER
1. What happened to Jenny?
2. Do you always want to do things your own way?
3. Does God want you to listen to what your friends and parents have to say?

A LITTLE PRAYER
Dear God, help me always to want your way and not just my own way.

A BIBLE VERSE FOR YOU TO LEARN
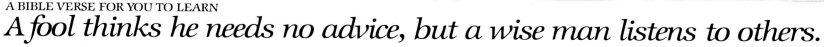
A fool thinks he needs no advice, but a wise man listens to others.

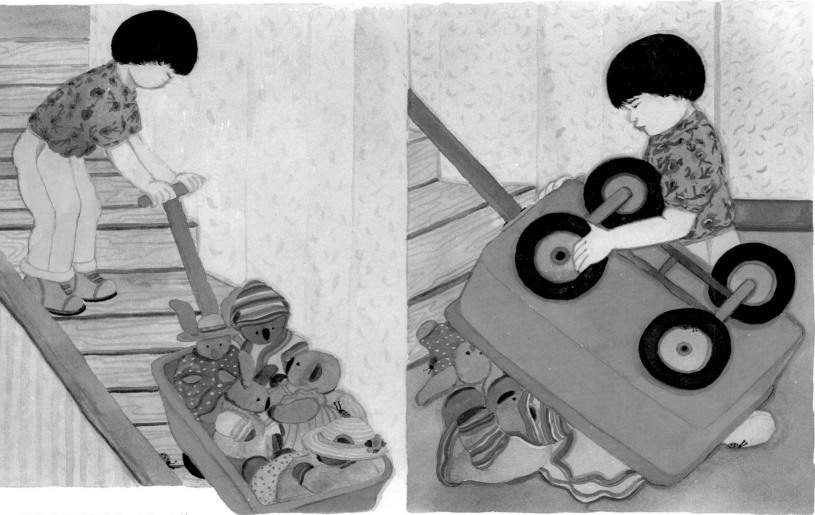

PROVERBS 12:15

The Bible is a special book.
It helps us to obey.
So read the Bible if you can,
A little every day.

In this picture, Lindsay and Stephen are listening to Bible stories. The other children are reading by themselves. They like to read stories from the Bible about Moses and King David and Esther. They expecially like the stories about Jesus and the wonderful things he did. Jesus made blind people see, and sick people well. Someday you will be able to read the Bible and read all of these things for yourself. That is something for you to look forward to.

SOME QUESTIONS TO ANSWER
1. What do we call God's special book?
2. Do you have a book of stories from the Bible? If not, ask your mother or father to get one for you.
3. Can you think of any stories from the Bible? Tell about one.

A LITTLE PRAYER
Dear God, thank you for the Bible. Help me to read it so I can know and do what you want me to.

A BIBLE VERSE FOR YOU TO LEARN
Despise God's Word and find yourself in trouble. Obey it and succeed.

PROVERBS 13:13

"Yes, I'll do it," said the boy,
"I'll do it right away."
But he forgot what he had said,
And he ran off to play.

Have I ever told you about a boy named Jamie? He had a "forgetter" in his head! He'd promise something and then forget about it. You could never believe him. His words didn't mean a thing. One day he promised to rake some leaves in the yard if his mother would let him play with his friends first. But she said, "No, I don't believe you. You have a hard time keeping your promises." So Jamie had to stay home to rake leaves. After that, Jamie learned to do what he promised. Now his mother believes him. She is happy, and he is happy, too. Remember always to keep your promises.

SOME QUESTIONS TO ANSWER
1. What did Jamie's mother want him to do?
2. Why wouldn't his mother let him play with his friends?
3. Can you think of something you said you would do but then didn't do?

A LITTLE PRAYER
Thank you, God, for always doing what you say. Help me always to keep my promises.

A BIBLE VERSE FOR YOU TO LEARN
God delights in those who keep their promises. PROVERBS 12:22

If you're acting naughty,
Your parents may spank you.
But when you get older,
You'll want to say, "Thank you!"

Oh my, what is happening to Little Bear? I think he was getting into the medicine cabinet. His mother told him not to, but he did it anyway. So now he is getting a spanking! Spankings and other kinds of punishment make you un-happy, but they also help you to be good. If your parents let you do bad things like lying and stealing and disobeying, you will probably grow up to be bad and unhappy. After you have been punished, your father and mother hug and kiss you. Then you feel good again, and you know that they love you. They want to keep you from being bad.

SOME QUESTIONS TO ANSWER
1. What did Little Bear do that was wrong?
2. Do you ever get punished? For what?
3. What are some ways your mother and father punish you?

A LITTLE PRAYER
Father in heaven, help me to obey and to be kind and good. Even though it hurts, thank you that I am punished when I disobey.

A BIBLE VERSE FOR YOU TO LEARN
Punishment that hurts chases evil from the heart. PROVERBS 20:30

Please have a little patience!
Don't push and kick and fight.
Sometimes you'll tire of waiting,
But you'll be doing right.

It isn't fun to wait and wait for your turn, but think what it would be like if everyone wanted to be first! There would be a lot of unhappiness and pushing and shoving and crying. In the picture you can see some children who are being patient and waiting for their turn. But I see two boys who aren't being patient at all. They are arguing over who should get the red car. If you were in the picture, what would you be doing? I hope you would be waiting patiently. God wants us to be patient and fair.

SOME QUESTIONS TO ANSWER
1. What are the children in the picture doing?
2. Which ones are arguing?
3. What should they do instead?

A LITTLE PRAYER
Dear Father in heaven, help me to learn to be patient and to wait for my turn.

A BIBLE VERSE FOR YOU TO LEARN
Be patient and you will finally win. PROVERBS 25:15

Don't say that someone did it
When you know it isn't true.
That's just as bad as hitting;
It's a thing you shouldn't do.

Oh, what is happening in the picture? First, Emily broke a cup and is trying to hide the pieces under the table. Can you see them there? Now she's pointing at Heather and saying that Heather broke the cup. Is that good? No, it is not good at all! If you break something and then say somebody else broke it, you are telling a lie and being very unfair to the other person. So if you break something, you should say, "I'm sorry. I did it." Be brave and say so when you have been careless, or done something wrong. God wants us to be brave and honest and fair.

SOME QUESTIONS TO ANSWER
1. Can you see someone in the picture who is telling a lie? What is her name?
2. What should you say to God if you tell a lie? What should you say to the other person?

A LITTLE PRAYER
Dear God, I am sorry if I have told lies. Help me always to tell the truth. I want to make you happy by doing what is right.

A BIBLE VERSE FOR YOU TO LEARN
Telling lies about someone is as harmful as hitting him. PROVERBS 25

See the children talk to God.
He likes it when we pray.
You can't see him, but he smiles
And hears you every day.

What is everyone doing in the picture? That's right, they are praying. They are talking to God. God is glad when you talk to him because he loves you. You talk to other people, so you should talk to God, too. He is right here in the room with you, even though you can't see him. What should you say to God? You can tell him you love him. You can thank him for all the good things he does for you. You can thank him for your parents and for your friends. You can tell him about your hurts. God is happy when you talk to him.

SOME QUESTIONS TO ANSWER
1. What are the children in the picture doing?
2. Does God like to hear you pray?
3. What are some things you can thank him for?

A LITTLE PRAYER
(say this silently in your heart without using your mouth)
Dear God, I love you. Help me to talk to you often.

A BIBLE VERSE FOR YOU TO LEARN
The Lord delights in the prayers of his people. PROVERBS 15:8

Be fair in everything you do;
Play fair in every game.
Don't mind at all
    if you should lose—
Be happy just the same.

Can you see the games the children are playing? Most of them are having a happy time. But I see something I don't like! In the center of the picture Jason is leaning over and peeking at someone else's cards! He's not playing fair. He's not playing by the rules. He is cheating. He wants to win more than he wants to do what is right. But God wants us to be fair, even if it means we will lose. If we win we must win fairly. So if you want to make God happy, don't cheat.

SOME QUESTIONS TO ANSWER
1. Point to Jason. What is he doing? Is he being fair?
2. Can you think of a time when you weren't being fair? Tell about it.
3. How can you make God happy when you play?

A LITTLE PRAYER
Dear Lord, please help me always to be fair and not to cheat.

A BIBLE VERSE FOR YOU TO LEARN
The Lord demands fairness. PROVERBS 16:11

Be careful, my children;
Don't go with a stranger.
His words may sound good,
But he might bring you danger.

Your parents have probably told you not to get into a car with a person you don't know. Do you know why? Because sometimes strangers who seem nice aren't nice at all. A stranger might say, "I will give you some candy if you ride with me in my car." Or he might say that he will show you his puppies or kittens. But don't do it. He might be a bad person who would hurt you if you went with him. The best thing to do is to run away from him. Don't stay and talk to him. The girl in the picture is running away from the man who offered her a lollipop. She is doing the right thing.

SOME QUESTIONS TO ANSWER
1. What is the girl in the picture doing?
2. What should you do if a stranger wants you to ride or walk with him?
3. What would you do if he said he would give you some candy? What if he wanted to show you his puppies or kittens?

A LITTLE PRAYER
Dear God, help me to listen to my parents and not to someone I don't know.

A BIBLE VERSE FOR YOU TO LEARN
Pretty words may hide a wicked heart. PROVERBS 26:23

Always be honest;
Don't cheat or lie.
Be truthful with others
And don't make them cry.

Justin was playing in the yard and found some money. He thought, *This is mine because I found it, and now I can buy some candy.* Just then Kristen came out of the house carrying her purple purse. She was crying. "I've lost my money. Have you seen it anywhere?" Justin thought about the yummy candy. "No, I haven't seen your money," he lied. Later Justin thought, *I shouldn't have said that.* He went into the house and said to Kristen, "I'm sorry," and then gave her the money he had found. She was glad because she had her money again, and God was glad because Justin had finally told the truth.

SOME QUESTIONS TO ANSWER
1. What did Justin find while he was playing?
2. What did he do with the money he found?
3. Can you think of a time you were honest even though it was hard?

A LITTLE PRAYER
Dear God, help me always to be honest.

A BIBLE VERSE FOR YOU TO LEARN
The Lord hates cheating and delights in honesty. PROVERBS 11:1

Can you do some things better
Than any other kid?
Remember, God is helping you,
So don't be acting big!

In the picture, Sarah is acting like she thinks she is better than all the other children. She thinks she is the best one in the class. Sometimes she even says, "I'm better than you are!" She is being selfish and proud. This is not good. Do you ever act like Sarah? If you do, please don't do it anymore. If you are especially good at coloring or tumbling or playing a game, remember it is because God is helping you. So don't be proud about it. That would make God sad. Say "Thank you" to God instead of thinking you're so great.

SOME QUESTIONS TO ANSWER
1. What is Sarah doing?
2. Can you do some things better than the other children can?
3. Should you be proud about it? Why not?

A LITTLE PRAYER
Father in heaven, thank you for the things I am good at doing. Thank you for helping me.

A BIBLE VERSE FOR YOU TO LEARN
Pride goes before a fall! PROVERBS 16:18

Who took care of Daddy
When he was just a lad?
Your grandma did, and grandpa too,
So show them you are glad.

In this picture you can see the children talking to their grandmother and grandfather. They are having a happy time. God wants you to make your grandparents happy because they took good care of your mother or father many years ago. You should say "Thank you" to your grandparents for all they have done. One good way of thanking them is to make them happy. You could write a letter or talk to them on the telephone. Maybe you can visit them or invite them to come and visit you. That will make them happy, and God will be happy too.

SOME QUESTIONS TO ANSWER
1. What do you call your grandparents?
2. How can you make your grandparents happy?
3. Why should we try to make our grandparents happy?

A LITTLE PRAYER
Dear God, thank you for my grandparents. Help me to make them happy.

A BIBLE VERSE FOR YOU TO LEARN
An old man's grandchildren are his crowning glory. PROVERBS 17:6

Getting mad is foolish.
It doesn't help a bit!
Instead, control your temper—
Don't kick or bite or hit!

In the picture you can see a boy named Adam. He was playing a table game with his sister, Meg. He didn't win, so he knocked the game off the table and is running into the other room. Now he won't play anymore. I think he is being a poor sport, don't you? He got mad about losing. But God doesn't want people to act that way. He wants us to learn to be happy even when we lose. In the other part of the picture you can see Adam being sorry about what he did. Now he is pushing Meg on the swing instead of being angry. Adam is learning to control his temper.

SOME QUESTIONS TO ANSWER
1. Why did Adam run away from his sister?
2. Was he being a good sport?
3. Does God want us to be happy even when we lose?

A LITTLE PRAYER
Father in heaven, please help me to be happy even when I lose.

A BIBLE VERSE FOR YOU TO LEARN
A wise man restrains his anger. PROVERBS 19:11

If you wake up really early
And your parents are asleep,
Be quiet as a little mouse—
And don't let out a peep!

Everyone in the picture is asleep except Kimberley. She woke up a long time before breakfast and before anyone else. Now she is quietly reading a book. She is as quiet as a little mouse because she knows the other people in the house want to sleep. She isn't playing with her drum or listening to the radio because she knows the loud sounds would wake everyone up. The next time you wake up early, pretend you are a little mouse! See how quiet you can be!

SOME QUESTIONS TO ANSWER
1. Do your parents like loud noise early in the morning?
2. What can you play with if you wake up early?
3. What little animal should you try to be like if you wake up early?

A LITTLE PRAYER
Dear God, thank you that I can rest when I am tired. But help me to be quiet when I wake up before anyone else.

A BIBLE VERSE FOR YOU TO LEARN
If you shout a pleasant greeting to a friend too early in the morning

he will count it as a curse! PROVERBS 27:14

Don't be mad
   when Mother scolds you;
Please don't fuss and pout.
It only means she wants to help,
Of that there is no doubt.

Why is Mother Bear unhappy with Little Bear? It is because Little Bear knocked all the oranges off the table. Can you see them on the floor? Mother Bear is telling Little Bear not to do it again. But I see something I don't like. Little Bear is pouting and sulking instead of saying, "I'm sorry, I won't do it again." If you do something wrong, admit it! Don't feel sorry for yourself if your mother needs to scold you. Be glad that she wants you to do what is right.

SOME QUESTIONS TO ANSWER
1. Why is Little Bear's mother scolding him?
2. Tell about a time you were scolded. Did you pout or become angry? What should you do instead?

A LITTLE PRAYER
Father in heaven, thank you for people who love me, who tell me to stop doing things that are wrong.

A BIBLE VERSE FOR YOU TO LEARN
It is a badge of honor to accept valid criticism. PROVERBS 25:12

Stephanie's having a party—
See all the children play.
For days and days she's
planned and planned;
What fun she'll have today!

What is happening in the picture? The children are having a party! What are the little bears doing? Everyone will have a good time. Whom do you think Stephanie invited to her party? I think she invited her friends. But she also invited some other children who just moved into the house down the street. She doesn't know them very well, but she wanted them to come, too. That was a nice thing for Stephanie to do. God likes us to be kind. He is happy with us when we do nice things for other people to make them happy.

SOME QUESTIONS TO ANSWER
1. Is there someone you don't know very well whom you could invite to a party? Who?
2. Think of a way besides having a party to make someone happy.

A LITTLE PRAYER
Dear God, thank you that I can do things to make other people happy.

A BIBLE VERSE FOR YOU TO LEARN
Joy fills hearts that are planning for good. PROVERBS 12:20

Taffy was a little bear
Who had a friend named Tad.
But once she said that Tad looked dumb,
And that made him feel sad.

Can you guess what the children and bears are doing?
They're getting ready for a play. It looks like everyone is
having a good time. But two of the bears are unhappy.
Taffy is pointing at Tad and said he looks dumb. Of course,
that hurt Tad's feelings. I think we should tell Taffy something important. Let's tell her, "Taffy, don't say things that
hurt other people's feelings. God wants us to be kind to
each other and to love each other." I hope Taffy tells Tad
she's sorry. Then Tad will feel better, and they will be
friends again.

SOME QUESTIONS TO ANSWER
1. What are the children and bears doing?
2. Should Taffy say unkind things to her friend?
3. Can God help Taffy tell Tad she's sorry? Can he help you
   when you are unhappy with someone?

A LITTLE PRAYER
Dear God, please help me to be kind to everyone, and to
like them.

A BIBLE VERSE FOR YOU TO LEARN
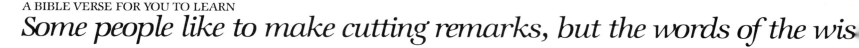
Some people like to make cutting remarks, but the words of the wis

soothe and heal. PROVERBS 12:18

Good is good and bad is bad,
And never the twain shall meet.
So do not say that bad is good,
Or that stealing can be neat.

Look what's happening in this picture! Joshua and Matt are taking Jeremy's bike while he isn't looking. That's not right. That's stealing! But that's not all. They're telling their friend Carlos that it's okay to steal. "It's fun to take things from other people. And besides, Jeremy can get another bike." But stealing makes God sad. And it makes God angry when someone tries to get others to be bad. I hope Carlos will be brave enough to tell his friends not to take the bike.

SOME QUESTIONS TO ANSWER
1. What are Joshua and Matt going to steal?
2. Jeremy isn't watching them, but Someone sees what they are doing. Do you know who it is?
3. Should you do what is wrong if your friends say it is okay?

A LITTLE PRAYER
Dear God, help me to say "No" when someone wants me to do something bad.

A BIBLE VERSE FOR YOU TO LEARN
The Lord despises those who say that bad is good, and good is bad

PROVERBS 17:15

Rebecca is a little girl
Who puts her toys away.
When Mother says, "Please do it now,"
Rebecca will obey.

This little girl's name is Rebecca. She is a happy little girl, but sometimes she doesn't like to put away her toys when it is time to go to bed! One day when a baby-sitter was taking care of her, she thought, *Tonight I won't need to put away my toys because my parents aren't home.* But then she thought, *I should do what my parents want me to, even though they aren't here.* So she is putting her toys away. Her parents will be happy when they come home and find everything put away. God is happy, too, because Rebecca is obeying her father and mother.

SOME QUESTIONS TO ANSWER
1. What is Rebecca doing?
2. What is something you can do to make your father and mother happy?
3. Does it make your parents happy when you obey them?

A LITTLE PRAYER
Dear God, help me to want to do whatever my parents tell me to.

A BIBLE VERSE FOR YOU TO LEARN
Give your parents joy. PROVERBS 23:25

Give thanks to God
For a father's love
And for his prayers
To heaven above.

In the picture you can see a father getting books from the library and reading to his children. You can see that the children like it when he reads to them. They know their father loves them, because he helps them and takes care of them. And I'll tell you a secret. Every day their father prays for them. God listens to his prayers and helps the children in many ways. He sends his angels to be with them, and he helps the children to be kind and good. Your father prays for you, and you should pray for him. Thank God every day for giving your father to you.

SOME QUESTIONS TO ANSWER
1. Maybe the father in the picture is reading one of the books you like. Which of your books do you think it might be?
2. When could you pray for your father and mother and brother or sister?

A LITTLE PRAYER
Dear Father in heaven, thank you for giving me a mother and father. Please help them to make me a good person, and help them to love you.

A BIBLE VERSE FOR YOU TO LEARN
A child's glory is his father. PROVERBS 17:6

Some boys and girls have many clothes,
And some don't have enough.
But we're not better if we own
A lot of toys and stuff.

Pretty clothes are nice, but not everybody has them. Some boys and girls come from families that don't have very much money. Their parents can't buy them new clothes and toys. Sometimes children who have lots of nice things act as if they are better than the children who don't have very much. But that is being foolish and unkind. If God gives you a lot of nice things, don't be proud about it. Instead, be thankful to God for giving you so much. And if your family does not have much money, you still have many things to be thankful for. And remember that God loves you just as much as he loves anyone.

SOME QUESTIONS TO ANSWER
1. Do you see the children in the picture whose clothes are not so pretty?
2. Does God love children more if they have lots of clothes and toys?
3. Does God love children just as much if they don't have lots of clothes and toys?

A LITTLE PRAYER
Father in heaven, thank you for all you have given me. Help me to like everyone I know, whether they are rich or poor.

A BIBLE VERSE FOR YOU TO LEARN
To despise the poor is to sin. Blessed are those who pity them.

PROVERBS 14:21

If you know what's right,
Don't do what is wrong,
No matter who says,
"It's okay, come along!"

Oh, Katie, don't do that! Can you see what she is doing? She is stealing a cookie. Her brother took one and said it was okay. Their mother said not to, but Katie is disobeying anyway. Katie is doing wrong just because her brother did! That is not good at all. When you know something is wrong, don't do it, even if someone else tells you it's okay. God is happy when you obey your parents and do what is right. He is unhappy when you listen to what you know is wrong.

SOME QUESTIONS TO ANSWER
1. Where are Katie and her family?
2. What is Katie doing with the cookie?
3. Should you ever say it's okay to do something you know is wrong?

A LITTLE PRAYER
Dear God, please help me always to do what I know is right and not listen to anyone who tries to get me to do something wrong.

A BIBLE VERSE FOR YOU TO LEARN
Stop listening to teaching that contradicts what you know is right.

PROVERBS 19:27

Little bears, stop fighting!
Will you never learn?
Please don't be so selfish—
Let others have a turn.

Oh, dear me! Look at the little bears. They are pushing and quarreling. They aren't being nice to each other at all. They both want to ride on the rocking horse. But neither of them can play with it while they are fighting. What should they do instead? That's right. They can take turns or even ride the horse together. They are being silly because they aren't sharing. Have you ever been foolish by fighting instead of sharing? I hope not, but if you have been, please don't be foolish anymore. Everyone should have a turn.

SOME QUESTIONS TO ANSWER
1. What are the bears fighting about?
2. What should they do instead of fighting?
3. Tell about a time you shared a toy with someone.

A LITTLE PRAYER
Father in heaven, please help me to share and not quarrel.

A BIBLE VERSE FOR YOU TO LEARN
It is an honor to stay out of a fight. Only fools insist on quarreling.

PROVERBS 20:3

Shut your eyes and hold them closed—
Now try to walk around.
Thank God for eyes that look and see
And ears that hear the sound.

In the picture you can see a little bear helping a lady cross the street. The lady can't see anything because she is blind. Shut your eyes and walk around, and you'll feel what it is like to be blind. Blind people live all their lives in darkness. But it is amazing how well they can walk around. Some use a white cane to help them feel if a table or chair is in their way, and some have a specially trained dog to guide them when they are outside. How thankful to God we should be because we can see and hear.

SOME QUESTIONS TO ANSWER
1. Can you point to the woman in the picture who is blind?
2. Why does she have a white cane?
3. Do you know anyone who is blind or who can't hear well?

A LITTLE PRAYER
Thank you so much, dear God, for eyes that see and ears that hear. Please help me to help anyone who can't see or hear as well as I do.

A BIBLE VERSE FOR YOU TO LEARN
If you have good eyesight and good hearing, thank God who gave them

to you. PROVERBS 20:12

ABOUT THE AUTHOR

Kenneth N. Taylor is best known as the translator of *The Living Bible*, but his first renown was as a writer of children's books. Ken and his wife, Margaret, have ten children, and his early books were written for use in the family's daily devotions. The manuscripts were ready for publication only when they passed the scrutiny of those ten young critics! Those books, which have now been read to two generations of children around the world, include *The Bible in Pictures for Little Eyes* (Moody Press), *Stories for the Children's Hour* (Moody Press), and *The Living Bible Story Book* (Tyndale House). Now the Taylor children are all grown, so *Wise Words for Little People*, *Big Thoughts for Little People*, and *Giant Steps for Little People* were written with the numerous grandchildren in mind.

Ken Taylor is a graduate of Wheaton College and Northern Baptist Seminary. He is the founder and chairman of Tyndale House Publishers. He and Margaret live in Wheaton, Illinois.

ABOUT THE ILLUSTRATOR

Kathryn E. Shoemaker has had broad experience as an art teacher, curriculum specialist, filmmaker, and illustrator. Her published works include twenty books, eight filmstrips, illustrations for many magazine articles, and numerous educational in-service materials. She is a strong advocate of the involvement of parents in the local schools, and spends a great deal of time as a volunteer in her children's school. She is also a volunteer with the Canadian Mental Health Association and the Red Cross.

Kathryn is a graduate of Immaculate Heart College in Los Angeles. She also studied at Chouinards Art Institute, Otis Art Institute, and Occidental College, and is a member of the Society of Illustrators. She and her two children, Kristen and Andrew, who helped critique the illustrations for the *Little People* books, live in Vancouver, British Columbia.